TUNE MY HEART

Tune My Heart

DAILY DEVOTIONS FROM
THE BELOVED HYMN,
"COME, THOU FOUNT OF
EVERY BLESSING"

Gwendolyn Harmon

Learning Ladyhood Press

Copyright © 2020 by Gwendolyn Harmon

All rights reserved. No part of this book may be reproduced in any manner whatsoever without written permission except in the case of brief quotations embodied in critical articles and reviews.

First Printing, 2020

All Scripture quoted is from the King James Version

Cover photos by Sherrilyn Shaw, used with permission

Contents

Preface		1
1	What Tunes My Heart?	3
2	The Need to Tune My Heart	5
3	Streams of Mercy	7
4	Learning the Songs of Heaven	9
5	Mount of God's Redeeming Love	11
6	Ebenezer	13
7	What is My Ebenezer?	15
8	God's Good Pleasure	17
9	Safely to Arrive at Home	19
10	Jesus Sought Me	21
11	To Rescue	23
12	How Great a Debtor	25
13	Bound by Goodness	27
14	Prone to Wander	29
15	Here's My Heart	31
16	Sealed for Courts Above	33

Preface

One of my favorite hymns over the years has been "Come, Thou Fount of Every Blessing". Its beautiful words were penned by Robert Robinson in the 1700s. In this hymn, Robinson's plea is for a heart tuned to sing of all the goodness and mercies of the Lord. Each of these short studies takes a line or two from Robinson's hymn and examines an aspect of tuning our hearts to sing God's grace. As you read through each of these studies, my prayer for you is that your heart will be tuned ever closer to the song of God's own heart.

"Come, Thou Fount of Every Blessing"

Come, Thou Fount of ev'ry blessing,
Tune my heart to sing Thy grace;
Streams of mercy, never ceasing,
Call for songs of loudest praise.
Teach me some melodious sonnet,
Sung by flaming tongues above;
Praise the mount —I'm fixed upon it—
Mount of Thy redeeming love.

Here I raise my Ebenezer—
Hither by Thy help I'm come;
And I hope by Thy good pleasure,
Safely to arrive at home.
Jesus sought me when a stranger,
Wand'ring from the fold of God;
He to rescue me from danger,
Interposed His precious blood.

O to grace how great a debtor
Daily I'm constrained to be!
Let Thy goodness, like a fetter,
Bind my wand'ring heart to Thee;
Prone to wander—Lord, I feel it—
Prone to leave the God I love;
Here's my heart—O take and seal it,
Seal it for Thy courts above.

Robert Robinson

1

What Tunes My Heart?

Come, Thou Fount of Every Blessing

The words of this hymn have been carefully crafted to express Biblical truths. We need our hearts tuned, and we need to keep our focus on God each day.

Hebrews 12:1-2 puts it this way: *"Wherefore seeing we also are compassed about with so great a cloud of witnesses, let us lay aside every weight, and the sin which doth so easily beset us, and let us run with patience the race that is set before us, Looking unto Jesus, the author and finisher of our faith; who for the joy that was set before Him endured the cross, despising the shame, and is set down at the right hand of the throne of God."*

Did you catch the three actions in this passage? *Lay aside* every "weight" (or distraction) and sin. *Run* with patience. *Look* to Jesus. These are the keys to having a heart tuned to sing God's grace. We must lay aside distractions, turn from sin, and live this life God has set before us with all our heart, keeping our eyes focused on Jesus.

"For consider Him that endured such contradiction of sinners against Himself, lest ye be wearied and faint in your minds. Ye have not yet resisted unto blood, striving against sin." (Hebrews 12:3-4)

When I fix my eyes upon Jesus, the temptations and trials I face pale in comparison with all that He went through on my behalf. With my eyes on Him, I can run with patience, knowing that my feet won't stumble over any patch of road rougher than His nail-pierced feet have walked.

Perhaps that is why Robert Robinson chose to begin his song with the words, "*Come,* Thou Fount of every blessing." God's presence is what tunes our hearts. We must simply keep our eyes fixed on the One who has promised never to leave us nor forsake us.

What is hindering you from enjoying God's presence today?

2

The Need to Tune My Heart

Tune my Heart to sing Thy Grace

The alarm buzzes. I groan and fumble around for the snooze button. Half an hour later, I groggily check the time on my phone, only to find that I accidentally turned the alarm off, and now I've overslept. I rush to get ready for day, trying to squeeze in my time with God without being late for work. I manage to leave just a few minutes late, only to hit a major traffic snarl. *Great. All that rushing, and I'm still going to be late.*

I spill my coffee getting out of the car, drop my keys just as I get to the door, and nearly fall over trying to balance the remains of my coffee and the stack of books I'm holding while trying to pick up my keys. I finally manage to straighten up, keys in hand, only to find that the door was unlocked the whole time.

Can you relate? Whether it's the rush to get to work on time, the small child waking you up at an obnoxiously early hour, or the hurried marathon of getting a family dressed, fed, and out the door to their various destinations, it can be all too easy to start the day off feeling stressed, harried, and not a bit like praising the Lord.

We need to be tuned. Think of a radio. In order to receive a specific signal, it needs to be tuned to the right frequency. Once it is tuned right, not only can it receive the signal, it can also broadcast the sounds carried by that signal for others to hear.

Our lives are full of distractions, and that is exactly why our hearts need to be "tuned": to be brought to the place where they will be able to receive God's grace, and then send back the praise God so rightly deserves from us. Once tuned, we can not only receive God's grace for the day, we can proclaim that grace to everyone we meet.

> *"Teach me Thy way, O Lord; I will walk in Thy truth:*
> *Unite my heart to fear Thy name"*
> *(Psalm 86:11)*

What distractions are keeping your heart from being "tuned in" to God's grace today?

3

Streams of Mercy

Streams of mercy, never ceasing,
Call for songs of loudest praise.

The remnant of the nation of Israel, newly returned from seventy years in exile, had gathered together. Fasting and wearing sackcloth, with dirt on their heads in deep mourning, they had assembled to worship. They listened as the Scriptures were read and they confessed their sins in prayer. Then, in the midst of their deep and solemn mourning over sin and petitions for God's forgiveness, several Levites got up and said loudly, for all to hear: *"Stand up and bless the Lord your God for ever and ever: and blessed be Thy glorious name, which is exalted above all blessing and praise"* (Nehemiah 9:5)

In the verses that follow, these Levites recount God's might, power, and faithfulness to His people. They extolled the justness of God's judgement and His faithfulness to warn them and to invite them to return to Him. Even when their rejection required that they be taken out of the land as God had warned, *"Nevertheless for Thy great mercies' sake Thou didst not utterly consume them, nor forsake them; for Thou art a gracious and merciful God."* (Nehemiah 9:31)

This remembrance of God's continual mercy led the people to dedicate themselves to the Lord in wholehearted service, offering back all He had given them in gratitude for His mercy.

When we look back on our lives, it is easy to find "streams of mercies" flooding our past. Times when God forgave, provided, healed, protected, or comforted, whether or not we "deserved" it. When we view our lives from the perspective of God's mercies, we cannot help but proclaim with the Psalmist,

> *"What shall I render unto the Lord*
> *for all His benefits toward me?"*
> *(Psalm 116:12)*

Often, what we view as our greatest trials are actually God's greatest mercies towards us. What does God want you to view through the lens of His mercy today?

4

Learning the Songs of Heaven

Teach me some melodious sonnet,
Sung by flaming tongues above

Growing up, these lines mystified me. What were the "flaming tongues" it referred to? Considering the words and their context, it seems there are two options: Either the "flaming tongues above" are a reference to Christians or angels praising God in heaven, or they are an allusion to the "tongues of fire" that appeared over the heads of the believers at Pentecost. (Acts 2) Either way, the plea remains the same. It is a plea to learn the songs of heaven; to be taught to worship God as He desires to be worshipped.

In Isaiah 6, the prophet Isaiah was allowed a peek into the very throne room of God, where seraphim cried one to another, *"Holy, holy, holy, is the Lord of hosts: the whole earth is full of His glory."(v.3)* Isaiah's response is characteristic of a heart confronted with the perfect holiness of God:

"Woe is me! For I am undone; because I am a man of unclean lips, and I dwell in the midst of a people of unclean lips; for my eyes have seen the King, the Lord of Hosts." (v.5)

When we catch a glimpse of God as He is, we can see ourselves as we truly are, and respond in contrite acknowledgement of just how short we fall of His holiness.

The book of Revelation gives us some further glimpses into the worship of God in heaven. In Revelation 4:8-11, the angelic beings say: *"Holy, holy, holy, Lord God Almighty, which was, and is, and is to come."*

Upon hearing this statement the four and twenty elders (saved humans now in heaven) fall down in worship, casting their crowns before the throne in humility, saying: *"Thou art worthy, O Lord, to receive glory and honour and power: for Thou hast created all things, and for Thy pleasure they are and were created."*

When our hearts are in tune with the holy God, we will naturally echo back His worthiness.

What song is your heart echoing back today?

5

Mount of God's Redeeming Love

Praise the mount, I'm fixed upon it—
Mount of Thy redeeming love.

When we have tuned our hearts to a view of God's holiness, we are inescapably reminded of our own sin. But for those who have trusted Christ for salvation, the remembrance of our sin recalls to our minds the greatness of God's forgiveness.

The mount of God's redeeming love is mount Calvary, where Jesus gave Himself a ransom for our sin. Christ took *our* sin on Himself, so that we might receive *His* righteousness in exchange. That in itself is enough to call forth songs of praises!

In Revelation 5:9-10, the elders sing of God's worthiness to open the seals and unleash God's righteous judgement because of the sacrifice He made in His redeeming love:

"And they sung a new song, saying, Thou art worthy to take the book, and to open the seals thereof: for Thou was slain, and hast redeemed us to God by Thy blood out of every kindred, and tongue, and people, and nation; and hast made us unto our God kings and priests: and we shall reign on the earth."

In response to this song of worship for God's redemption, a multitude bursts out in praise, saying,

"Worthy is the Lamb that was slain to receive power, and riches, and wisdom, and strength, and honour, and glory, and blessing." (v.12) And at this, *every* creature responds: *"Blessing, and honour, and glory, and power, be unto Him that sitteth upon the throne, and unto the Lamb for ever and ever." (v.13)*

When our hearts are tuned to the praise of God's redeeming love, we will be filled with the joy of God's salvation. We will burst out in songs of praise, for His redeeming love has demonstrated once and for all that He indeed is worthy.

What does Jesus' redeeming sacrifice on Calvary mean for you today?

6

Ebenezer

Here I raise mine Ebenezer

It had been a dark time for Israel. They had gone to battle against the Philistines and been horrifically defeated. There were many casualties, and, perhaps the worst of all, the ark of the covenant had been taken. They had brought it to battle presumptuously, treating it like a lucky charm. Now, their symbol of God's presence had been lost.

But God was still at work. While the ark was in the hands of the Philistines, He repeatedly displayed His power. In the end, the frightened Philistines put the ark on a cart and sent it back to Israel.

How excited the Israelites must have been to see it! But then, a crowd gathered and became curious about what might be inside the ark. Instead of treating the ark as holy, they opened the ark and looked inside, contrary to God's clear instructions. God judged them for their disobedience. The ark was back, but all was not well between God and His people.

For twenty years Israel mourned, then Samuel spoke up, showing them the way back to God: *"If ye do return unto the Lord with all your hearts, then put away the strange gods and Ashtaroth from among you, and prepare your hearts unto the Lord, and serve Him only: and He will deliver you out of the hand of the Philistines."* (I Samuel 7:3)

Israel did, and God Himself won an astounding victory over their enemies. After the battle, Samuel *"took a stone, and set it between Mizpeh and Shen, and called the name of it Eben-ezer, saying, Hitherto hath the Lord helped us."* (I Samuel 7:12) The name Ebenezer means "stone of the help". Every time the Israelites saw that stone, they were reminded of God's glorious working on their behalf.

God's Word is full of such examples of God at work on behalf of His children. To tune our hearts, we can remember the great things God has done for His children all across history.

What "Ebenezer" account in Scripture resonates the most with your heart?

7

What is My Ebenezer?

Hither by Thy help I'm come

Remembering the great things God has done for His people throughout Scripture can indeed tune our hearts to praise God, but an even more powerful way to tune our hearts is to remember the great things God has done for us *personally.*

The hymn writer echoes Samuel's words "Hitherto hath the Lord helped us." The Ebenezer stone was placed in a location where God had led them to victory. For the saved in Christ, we each have our own victories to remember. Even when we feel the most defeated or hopeless, we can always remember that God saved us. He won that victory, and can help us win every other victory the same way: by His grace. It is His grace that enables us to choose to say "yes" to God and "no" to sin. It is His grace that *has* delivered and it is His grace that *will* deliver.

To tune our hearts to our own "Ebenezers," we look back on our lives to see the times when God has shown Himself strong on our behalf; when He has displayed His faithfulness and mercy where we least deserved it. There may be many, but often, there is one that stands out from the others.

Perhaps David was thinking of his own Ebenezer when he penned Psalm 40, which begins:

"I waited patiently for the Lord; and He inclined unto me, and heard my cry. He brought me up also out of an horrible pit, out of the miry clay, and set my feet upon a rock, and established my goings." (v.1-2)

Notice in the next verse that the result of deliverance is praise: *"And He hath put a new song in my mouth, even praise unto our God: many shall see it, and fear, and shall trust in the Lord." (v.3)*

Think back through your life and ask the Holy Spirit to show you: what are your Ebenezers?

8

God's Good Pleasure

And I hope, by Thy good pleasure,

The phrase "Thy good pleasure" speaks to the sovereignty of God. Jesus told His disciples: *"Fear not, little flock; for it is your Father's good pleasure to give you the kingdom." (Luke 12:32)* He can give the kingdom, because it is His to give, and He is pleased to give it!

Ephesians 1:5-6 speaks to another gift of God's good pleasure: *"Having predestinated us unto the adoption of children by Jesus Christ to Himself, according to the good pleasure of His will, To the praise of the glory of His grace, wherein He hath made us accepted in the beloved."*

Notice that the gift of adoption, of becoming a child of God, brings praise to God for His grace. Ephesians 1:9-12 says similarly,

"Having made known unto us the mystery of His will, according to His good pleasure which He hath purposed in Himself: That in the dispensation of the fulness of times He might gather together in one all things in Christ, both which are in heaven, and which are in earth; even in Him: In whom also we

have obtained an inheritance, being predestinated according to the purpose of Him who worketh all things after the counsel of His own will: That we should be to the praise of His glory, who first trusted in Christ."

Philippians 2:13 says, *"For it is God which worketh in you both to will and to do of His good pleasure."* and in 2 Thessalonians 1:11-12 Paul prays, *"that our God would count you worthy of this calling, and fulfil all the good pleasure of His goodness, and the work of faith with power: That the name of our Lord Jesus Christ may be glorified in you, and ye in Him, according to the grace of our God and the Lord Jesus Christ."*

All that we are, all that we have, our very ability to serve Him: it is all of grace, bestowed of God's good pleasure.

***Take a moment to ponder these gifts of God's good pleasure.
What else has God given you?***

9

Safely to Arrive at Home

And I hope, by Thy good pleasure,
Safely to arrive at home

This world is truly not our home. As Christians, we are citizens of heaven, waiting to be welcomed to the glories of our eternal home. And while we wait, we are to work, seeking to glorify God through our time on earth.

But as we live in this world, it is easy to become so consumed with looking at the ground beneath our feet that we lose sight of where we're heading. That is why it is helpful to tune our hearts to praise and thank God for the glorious home He has prepared for us.

"And I saw a new heaven and a new earth: for the first heaven and the first earth were passed away; and there was no more sea. And I John saw the holy city, new Jerusalem, coming down from God out of heaven, prepared as a bride adorned for her husband. And I heard a great voice out of heaven saying, Behold, the tabernacle of God is with men, and He will dwell with them, and they shall be His people, and God Himself shall be with them, and be their

God. And God shall wipe away all tears from their eyes; and there shall be no more death, neither sorrow, nor crying, neither shall there be any more pain: for the former things are passed away." (Revelation 21:1-4)

"And I saw no temple therein: for the Lord God Almighty and the Lamb are the temple of it. And the city had no need of the sun, neither of the moon, to shine in it: for the glory of God did lighten it, and the Lamb is the light thereof." (Revelation 21:22-23)

This is our destination. The glories of heaven are the greatest gift of God's good pleasure, and they wait for us, just around the bend.

What aspect of heaven do you look forward to the most?

10

Jesus Sought Me

Jesus sought me when a stranger,
Wandering from the fold of God

If you were saved as a teen or adult, you probably remember how it was when you were far from God, and how He sought you. Perhaps you were saved as a young child, as I was, and don't really remember a time before salvation. Either way, the truth remains: Jesus sought us.

Romans 5:8 says, *"But God commendeth His love toward us, in that, while we were yet sinners, Christ died for us."* Before you and I had even breathed our first breath, Christ had already taken our sins upon Him and paid our debt. That is how much He loves us.

Jesus said, *"For the Son of man is come to seek and to save that which was lost." (Luke 19:10)* God Himself chose to leave the glories of heaven and put on human flesh, just to save us from our sins. Philippians 2 describes it this way:

"Who, being in the form of God, thought it not robbery to be equal with God: But made Himself of no reputation, and took upon Him the form of a

servant, and was made in the likeness of men: And being found in fashion as a man, He humbled Himself, and became obedient unto death, even the death of the cross." (v.5-7)

Jesus humbled Himself to reconcile us, even though we had done nothing worthy of His mercy or His love. Isaiah 64: 6 says that *"all our righteousnesses are as filthy rags."* Even on our best day, we could not have deserved to be reconciled with a perfectly holy God. But despite our unworthiness, Christ still gave Himself, and we still can be reconciled with that same perfectly holy God. Colossians 1:21 says *"And you, that were sometime alienated and enemies in your mind by wicked works, yet now hath He reconciled..."*

Gratefulness for our own reconciliation should prompt us to seek others, as God sought us, that they too would be reconciled with God. Consider 2 Corinthians 5:18, which says that God has given us *"the ministry of reconciliation."* That is why we are here.

> ***Today as you thank God for seeking you, who does He want you to seek for Him?***

11

To Rescue

He to rescue me from danger
Interposed His precious blood.

We don't hear the word "interposed" very much anymore. It means to come between, and has the idea of mediating or stepping in to reconcile. That is what Christ did for us. His blood was interposed, or placed between us and God so that we could be reconciled to God and rescued from an eternity in hell.

But just as it can be easy to forget the glories of heaven towards which we journey, it is equally as easy to forget the misery from which we have been spared. It is good to be reminded of this, though; because the misery we have been rescued from is the misery to which the unsaved multitudes around us are still headed.

Three times in Mark 9, Jesus describes Hell as a place *"where their worm dieth not, and the fire is not quenched."* (v. 44, 46, 48) In the account of the rich man and Lazarus, Jesus describes Lazarus *"in torments"* and tells of how he begs just for a drop of water to cool his tongue. (Luke 16: 23-24) In the same account, it is said that there is *"a great gulf fixed"* that none can cross –once there, one can never leave. The torments of burning, decay, and unquenchable thirst are unending, unrelenting, and inescapably permanent.

But then, Jesus stepped between you and eternal torment. He has *"washed us from our sins in His own blood" (Revelation 1:5)* and rescued us from the unending punishment we rightly deserved. The just wrath of the holy God was appeased when Christ, God in the flesh, took the sentence we had earned and paid it Himself with His own sinless blood.

Thus, you and I, once hell-bound sinners, can now stand before the just and holy God in spotless robes of Christ's righteousness, having been rescued from hell once and for all.

Christ holds the keys of death and hell. (Rev. 1:18)
What does that mean for you?

12

How Great a Debtor

O to grace, how great a debtor
Daily I'm constrained to be!

Grace. It's a word that has been bandied about by Christians in all sorts of ways, with all sorts of meanings. But notice the hymnist's words: he speaks of being *in debt* to grace.

Our salvation is of grace, not works. (Ephesians 2:8-9) It is not the keeping of the law that saves us. But while grace frees us from being servants of sin, it necessarily leads us into service to God, which entails acting in accordance with His righteousness.

Romans 6:15 explains: *"What then? Shall we sin, because we are not under the law, but under grace? God forbid. Know ye not, that to whom ye yield yourselves servants to obey, his servants ye are to whom ye obey; whether of sin unto death, or of obedience unto righteousness"*

Grace frees us to obey God and live in righteousness. Having been freed from sin, we now have the ability to say "yes" to God and "no" to sin. Titus 2: 11-14 gives a full and beautiful picture of how this works:

"For the grace of God that bringeth salvation hath appeared to all men, Teaching us that, denying ungodliness and worldly lusts, we should live soberly, righteously, and godly, in this present world; Looking for that blessed hope and the glorious appearing of the great God and our Savior Jesus Christ; Who gave Himself for us, that He might redeem us from all iniquity, and purify unto Himself a peculiar people, zealous of good works."

Christ gave Himself to rescue us, and asks daily obedience, not just for His own glory, but for our good as well. He knows the destruction that sin inevitably causes in the life of a believer (or an unbeliever, for that matter.) That is why He saved us.

What is the Holy Spirit offering you grace to say no to today?

13

Bound by Goodness

Let Thy goodness, like a fetter,
Bind my wandering heart to Thee

The goodness of God is one of the foundations of our faith. If God were not perfectly good, we could not trust Him, neither would He be just or holy. The truth of God's goodness does indeed bind our hearts to Him in faith and trust.

The word fetter is another word we hear less of these days. It means a chain or restraint, specifically for the feet. The hymnist gives us a good picture of what he is asking of God: It would be hard to wander very far from anything one's feet are chained to!

A heart in tune with God will desire to be ever nearer to Him. For us as Christians, whom God has promised never to leave or forsake (Hebrews 13:5), any distance between us and God is purely self-inflicted. The hymnist is begging to be tethered to God by His goodness.

This is a Biblical plea. Romans 2:4 says that *"the goodness of God leadeth thee to repentance."* Just as Isaiah was caused to see the depth of his own sinfulness when he was confronted with the holiness of God, a glimpse of God's goodness to us causes us to see just how undeserving we are. When we are wandering, God's goodness calls us back.

David, in Psalm 23 states that *"Surely goodness and mercy shall follow me all the days of my life: and I will dwell in the house of the Lord for ever."* When our hearts are tuned, we can turn and see God's goodness to us in every step we have taken. It is as if we are surrounded by God's goodness every moment. Our hearts will echo the cry of another psalmist:

"Oh that men would praise the Lord for His goodness, and for His wonderful works to the children of men!" (Psalm 107:8)

How has God been good to you today?

14

Prone to Wander

Prone to wander –Lord, I feel it—
Prone to leave the God I love

Did you ever get lost in a store as a child? I remember the absolute terror when, after being told not to wander off, I had wandered just a *little* too far and didn't notice when my mom turned the corner into the next aisle. All of a sudden, I couldn't see her. I felt frightened, unprotected, and alone.

Wandering from God causes the same feelings. When I am far from God, things frighten me which God never intended me to fear. I face attacks from the enemy unprotected by the shield of God's grace I have intentionally left behind. When I am far from God I feel alone, when, if I would only turn to seek Him, He is right there.

The truth is, we are all prone to wander. I once heard the Christian life described as an upward climb on a downward escalator. We can only keep going the right direction if we keep going. As soon as we stop moving forward, the world, the flesh, and the devil pull us back. Paul puts it this way:

"Brethren, I count not myself to have apprehended: but this one thing I do, forgetting those things which are behind, and reaching forth unto those things which are before, I press toward the mark for the prize of the high calling of God in Christ Jesus." (Philippians 3:13-14)

The way to keep from wandering is to tune our hearts to press forward in Christ,

"Holding forth the word of life; that I may rejoice in the day of Christ, that I have not run in vain, neither laboured in vain." (Philippians 2:16)

It's hard to wander off when your eyes are fixed upon God!

How is God asking you to press forward with Him today?

15

Here's My Heart

Here's my heart— O take and seal it

What do your treasure most? Jesus said, *"Where your treasure is, there will your heart be also." (Matthew 6:21)* If we are to have hearts tuned to sing God's praise, we must do as Colossians 3:1-2 says:

"If ye then be risen with Christ, seek those things which are above, where Christ sitteth on the right hand of God. Set your affection on things above, not on things on the earth."

If our "treasure," that which is most precious to us, consists of earthly things, our affections (our hearts) are in the wrong place.

The ancient commandment of *"Thou shalt love the Lord thy God with all Thy heart, and with all thy soul, and with all thy might"* was not abolished by the new covenant. In fact, Jesus said that this was the first, or most foundational commandment. (Mark 12:30) But to love God this way requires submission.

Jesus is the ultimate example of this. In John 6:38 He says, *"For I came down from heaven, not to do Mine own will, but the will of Him that sent Me."* And on the very eve of His crucifixion, He prayed, *"not my will, but Thine, be done." (Matthew 22:42)* While displaying a human desire to escape the intense suffering He knew was coming, He demonstrated a sinless heart of submission to God's will, whatever the cost.

That is where our hearts should be. A heart tuned to sing of God's goodness, mercy, grace, or anything else will recognize that His will is *"good, and acceptable, and perfect." (Romans 12:2)*

With our hearts tuned, we will treasure God's will as our highest goal, and trust Him to bring our desires in line with His own. We will surrender all our earthly treasures to Him, all our hopes, dreams, and ambitions, that He might be the only treasure that holds our hearts.

What treasure holds your heart today?

16

Sealed for Courts Above

Here's my heart— O take and seal it,
Seal it for Thy courts above.

When Robert Robinson penned these words in the eighteenth century, envelopes as we know them were not yet in use. Whenever he finished writing a letter, he would fold the paper or papers and drip wax from a candle onto the seam to stick the pages together. Then, if he were anyone of importance, he would press a ring or stamp into the wax to give it his "seal."

Wax seals were also used to verify the identity of the signer on important documents. From ancient times on, the seal of a ruler or a person of great social standing was not to be broken without that person's permission. (Think of Caesar's seal on the tomb of Jesus in Matthew 27.)

As Christians, we are sealed by God. Ephesians 1:13 says,

"In whom [Christ] ye also trusted, after that ye heard the word of truth, the gospel of your salvation: in whom also after that ye believed, ye were sealed

with that Holy Spirit of promise, which is the earnest of our inheritance until the redemption of the purchased possession, unto the praise of His glory."

The Holy Spirit is our seal. It is the proof of our identity in Christ and our inheritance to come. This is a greater truth than we often recognize.

Since God Himself has sealed us, and God Himself (the Holy Spirit) *is* the seal, nothing less than God Himself can break it. That means that nothing less than God Himself could take away our salvation, and He never will.

"For I am persuaded, that neither death, nor life, nor angels, nor principalities, nor things present, nor things to come, nor height, nor depth, nor any other creature, shall be able to separate us from the love of God, which is in Christ Jesus our Lord." (Romans 8:38-39)

Is your heart tuned to the truth of your security in Christ?

www.ingramcontent.com/pod-product-compliance
Lightning Source LLC
Chambersburg PA
CBHW071506080526
44587CB00016B/2713